PENGUINS

alex kuskowski

Consulting Editor, Diane Craig,
M.A./Reading Specialist

Sandcastle

An Imprint of Abdo Publishing
www.abdopublishing.com

visit us at www.abdopublishing.com

Published by Abdo Publishing, a division of ABDO, PO Box 398166, Minneapolis, Minnesota 55439.
Copyright © 2015 by Abdo Consulting Group, Inc. International copyrights reserved in all countries.
No part of this book may be reproduced in any form without written permission from the publisher.
SandCastle™ is a trademark and logo of Abdo Publishing.

Printed in the United States of America, North Mankato, Minnesota
062014
092014

Editor: Liz Salzmann
Content Developer: Nancy Tuminelly
Cover and Interior Design: Anders Hanson, Mighty Media, Inc.
Photo Credits: Shutterstock

Library of Congress Cataloging-in-Publication Data
Kuskowski, Alex., author.
  Penguins / Alex Kuskowski.
     pages cm. -- (Zoo animals)
  Audience: 004-009.
  ISBN 978-1-62403-274-5
  1. Penguins--Juvenile literature. I. Title.
  QL696.S47K87 2015
  598.47--dc23

                              2013041835

SandCastle™ Level: Transitional

SandCastle™ books are created by a team of professional educators, reading specialists, and content developers
around five essential components—phonemic awareness, phonics, vocabulary, text comprehension, and fluency—to
assist young readers as they develop reading skills and strategies and increase their general knowledge. All books
are written, reviewed, and leveled for guided reading, early reading intervention, and Accelerated Reader® programs
for use in shared, guided, and independent reading and writing activities to support a balanced approach to literacy
instruction. The SandCastle™ series has four levels that correspond to early literacy development. The levels are
provided to help teachers and parents select appropriate books for young readers.

EMERGING · BEGINNING · **TRANSITIONAL** · FLUENT

CONTENTS

PENGUINS

Penguins are birds.

People see penguins at the zoo.

AT THE ZOO

Penguins at the zoo live in a pen. They have ice. They have water.

PENGUIN FEATURES

Penguins have white stomachs.
Their backs are black.

Penguins have **flippers.**
Flippers help penguins
swim fast.

11

A group of penguins is a colony. Some colonies have thousands of penguins.

FOOD

In the wild, penguins hunt for food underwater. At zoos, penguins are given fish to eat.

PENGUIN CHICKS

Penguins lay eggs.
Chicks grow in the
eggs. Then they **hatch**.

PENGUIN FUN

Some penguins slide on their stomachs. They move fast.

Penguins clean
their feathers.
Penguins help
clean each other.

FAST FACTS

- Penguins have more feathers than most other birds.

- Penguins cannot fly.

- Emperor penguins are the largest type of penguin.

- Penguins **molt** all their feathers at the same time.

QUICK QUIZ

1. Penguins have white stomachs.
    True or False?

2. Penguins live in colonies.
    True or False?

3. At zoos, penguins are fed plants.
    True or False?

4. Penguins do not clean their
    feathers. *True or False?*

GLOSSARY

flipper - a wide, flat limb of a sea creature, such as a seal or a dolphin, that is used for swimming.

hatch - to break out of an egg.

molt - to shed feathers, fur, or another body covering.